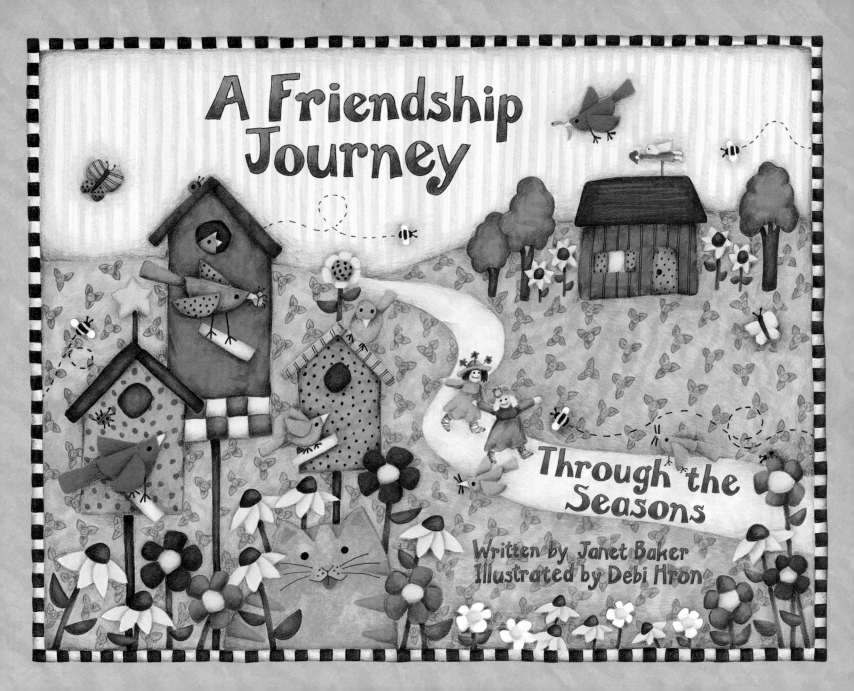

A Friendship Journey

Through the Seasons

Written by Janet Baker
Illustrated by Debi Hron

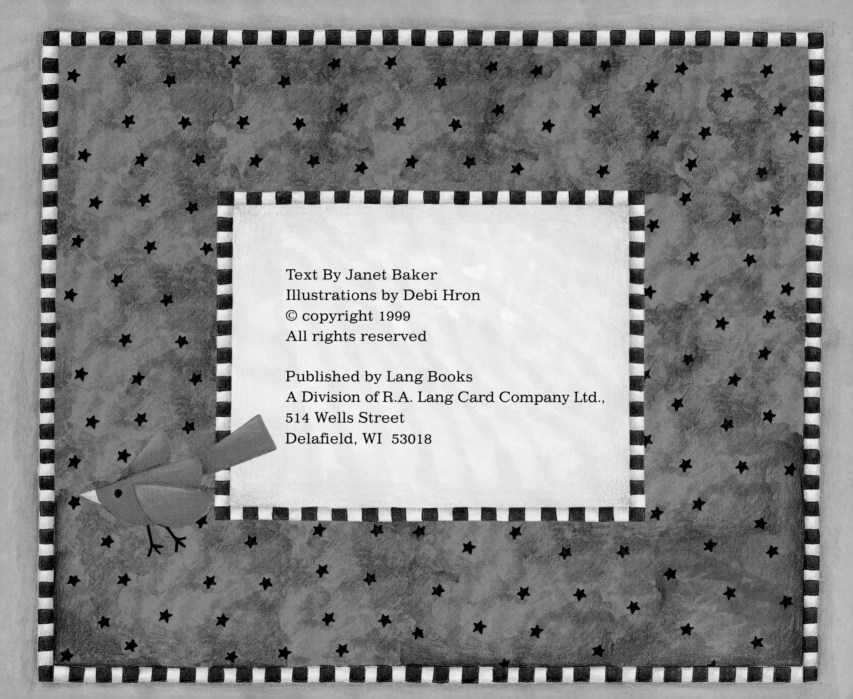

Text By Janet Baker
Illustrations by Debi Hron
© copyright 1999

Published by Lang Books
A Division of R.A. Lang Card Company Ltd.,
514 Wells Street
Delafield, WI 53018

Artful Experiences for Friends and Family

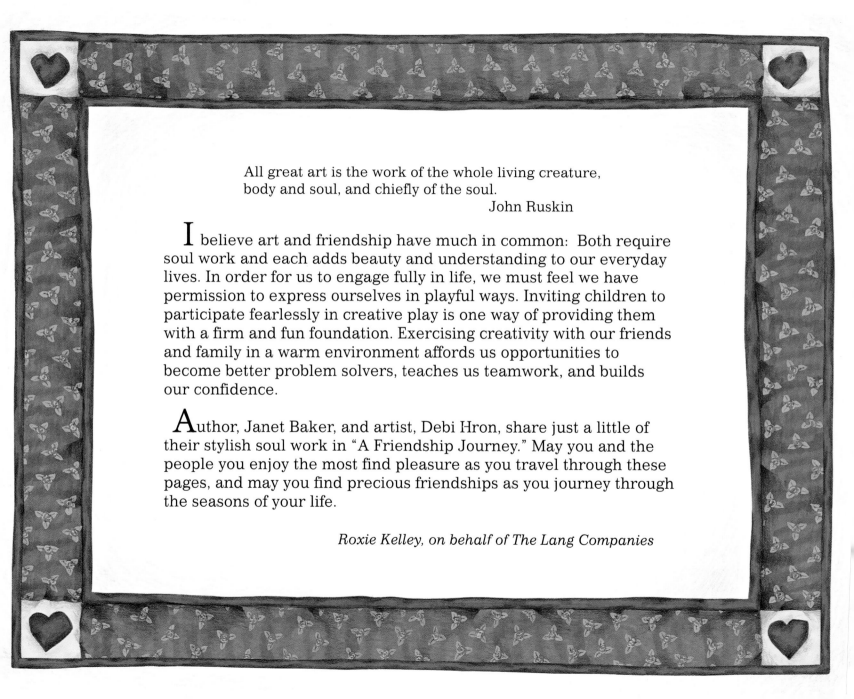

All great art is the work of the whole living creature,
body and soul, and chiefly of the soul.
John Ruskin

I believe art and friendship have much in common: Both require
soul work and each adds beauty and understanding to our everyday
lives. In order for us to engage fully in life, we must feel we have
permission to express ourselves in playful ways. Inviting children to
participate fearlessly in creative play is one way of providing them
with a firm and fun foundation. Exercising creativity with our friends
and family in a warm environment affords us opportunities to
become better problem solvers, teaches us teamwork, and builds
our confidence.

Author, Janet Baker, and artist, Debi Hron, share just a little of
their stylish soul work in "A Friendship Journey." May you and the
people you enjoy the most find pleasure as you travel through these
pages, and may you find precious friendships as you journey through
the seasons of your life.

Roxie Kelley, on behalf of The Lang Companies

To
Wonderfully wise Whitney,
Beautifully beloved Blaire,
Happy heavenly Haley,
and
Herb
(my forever Valentine).
I cherish you all.
JB

To My Mother,
who nurtured, coached, nudged and loved me
through each step of my journey.
DH

Spring

The blanket of winter is pulled back for us to glimpse the first color coming up through the ground. Our journey takes us where the miracle of new life continues when the freshness of spring comes into full bloom.
Come, let's celebrate spring!

Hold fast your dreams within your heart
Keep one still, secret spot
Where dreams may go and sheltered so,
May thrive and grow where doubt and fear are not.
Oh, keep a place
Apart within your heart
For little dreams to go.

~Louise Driscoll

Memory Pillow

My three daughters have t-shirts that hold such sweet memories that they want to keep them forever. Here is a great way to transform those shirts into a keepsake sleepover pillow.

Select the t-shirt you want to use as the main body of the pillow. Cut some of the sleeves and bottom of the shirt off.

Following the package directions on the fusible webbing, iron it on the back of the second shirt's design. Cut out the design and iron it on the front of the first shirt.

Turn shirt inside out and using a running stitch, sew up the arms and bottom, leaving the neck open, turn right side out again.

Stuff the pillow shirt with pillow stuffing full enough to keep its shape. Stitch up the neck, using a running stitch.

Things You'll Need:

Old shirt
  (no holes & little or
  no design on front)
Old shirt with favorite
  design on front
Scissors
Fusible webbing
Iron
Needle
Sewing thread
Pillow stuffing

The only thing to do is to hug one's friends tight and do one's job.

Edith Wharton

Things You'll Need:

1 dowel rod ¼" in
  diameter cut into
  a 15" piece
14 gauge wire
20 gauge copper
  wire
Wire cutters
Needle nose pliers
Decorative beads

You never know
when someone may
catch a dream
from you.

Helen Lowrie Marshall

Bubble Wands

Bend the 14 gauge wire around one end of the dowel rod about seven times and then wrap it around a bead ½" or larger, Place the end of the wire up through the hole in the bead so it's in there snugly.

At the top of the dowel rod, lay one inch of the 14 gauge wire on the rod. Using the wire cutters to help, bend the wire in whatever shape you have in mind (star, heart, house, butterfly...). Continuing with the wire that is now a design, wrap the wire around the dowel rod and the one inch of wire securely about ten times. Cut and bend the wire flat to the dowel.

Now for the fun part! Cut a piece of the wire to cross through your design. Slide a bead through it and wrap it on either side around the outside wire. This will keep your wand secure. Using the copper wire, wrap the end around one side of your design a few times, slide it through the bead and wrap around the other side and cut. Do the same thing again with the copper wire to give your Bubble Wand an "artsy look".

Bubble Solution:
2 cups Dawn dishwashing liquid
6 cups water
¾ cup corn syrup

Mix ingredients and pour into a shallow container that is larger than your wand face.

I meant to do my work today-
But a brown bird sang in the apple tree,
And a butterfly flitted across the field,
And all the leaves were calling me.

And the wind went sighing over the land,
Tossing the grasses to and fro,
And a rainbow held out its shining hand-
So what could I do but laugh and go?

Richard LeGallienne

Jelly Bellies

Cut two squares of felt, 4" x 4". Read the package directions on the fusible webbing and with help from an adult, iron it on one of the felt squares. Iron the two pieces of felt together so the fusible webbing "glues" the two pieces together. Cut out the body from this felt.

Then cut out a pocket (using pattern from below) from another piece of felt.

Sew pocket to front of chick with a small running stitch or glue together. (If you use glue, let it dry.)

Refer to pattern and paint a small black dot with the fabric paint and let it dry.

Thread a large needle with the ribbon. Pull the ribbon through the felt where the "X" is on the pattern. This creates a loop for hanging.

Fill the pocket with mini jelly beans.

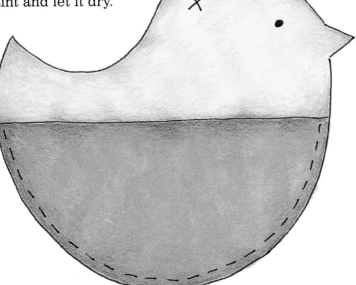

Things You'll Need:

Felt (spring colors)
Fusible webbing
Sewing thread
Needle
Pastel colored ribbon for hanging
Tracing paper and pencil
Black fabric paint for eyes
Scissors
Iron

These would make great spring party favors for your class when the pockets are filled with mini jelly beans.

I still find each day too short for all the
thoughts I want to think, all the walks
I want to take, all the books I want to read,
and all the friends I want to see.

John Burroughs

A Friendship Journal

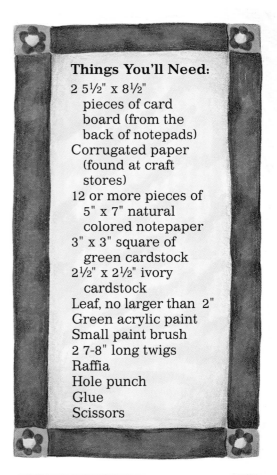

Brush the glue on one side of the two pieces of cardboard. Cover with the corrugated paper and allow to dry. Punch a hole 2½" from the top and 2½" from the bottom. Repeat with the other piece. The corrugated paper will then be the front and back cover of your journal.

Paint one side of the leaf and carefully lay it on the ivory paper. Gently rub over the leaf so the paint is transferred to the paper. Making sure the leaf does not move. Remove the leaf. Allow to dry.

Glue the green cardstock to the center of the corrugated paper. Center, and glue the ivory paper to the green paper.

Punch holes in the notepaper to match the holes in the covers. Lay the twigs across the left side, one under the back cover and one on top of the front cover. Thread about 10" of the raffia around the bottom twig, through the holes in the paper and the covers. Tie in a bow around the twig on top.

Things You'll Need:
2 5½" x 8½" pieces of card board (from the back of notepads)
Corrugated paper (found at craft stores)
12 or more pieces of 5" x 7" natural colored notepaper
3" x 3" square of green cardstock
2½" x 2½" ivory cardstock
Leaf, no larger than 2"
Green acrylic paint
Small paint brush
2 7-8" long twigs
Raffia
Hole punch
Glue
Scissors

Take a friend on a nature walk to collect what you need to make your journal...
Make an extra for another friend!

May Day is the truest form of celebration of Spring! Countries have been celebrating the reappearance of flowers and new life for centuries in a variety of ways.

The joy of being outside after the stillness of winter is reason enough to dance. A Maypole, with it's festive ribbons, brings spring alive through movement and laughter.

May Day Baskets

May baskets are a wonderful way to share the miracle of spring with special people.

Cut the paper into a 12" square. Roll and glue side and bottom edge to form a cone shape. Allow to dry. Glue ends of the ribbon to each side of the cone to form a handle.

Place the flowers you've selected inside the cone. Go to the home of a friend or neighbor and hang the basket on the front door knob. Ring the door bell and do one of two things:

Hide behind bushes or around the corner of the house. When the door is opened, jump out and yell, "May Day!" or...

Run away as soon as you ring the doorbell so no one sees you. You will know that you've made someone feel very special!

Things You'll Need:

Colored Paper
Scissors
Glue
Ribbon
Fresh or fabric flowers
Wire cutters

Those who wish to sing always find a song.

Swedish Proverb

Friendship consists in forgetting
what one gives, and remembering
what one receives.

Alexandre Dumas (1802-1870)

A Gift of Soothing Bath Salts

Paint the clay pot and saucer inside and out and set aside to dry. Place a dab of another color paint on a disposable plate. When the pot and saucer are dry, dip the heart shaped sponge into the dab of paint gently, covering the heart completely but not too wet.

Lightly sponge around the pot and saucer, adding more paint to sponge when necessary. Allow to dry. Spray with clear varnish, inside and out, and let dry.

Mix Epsom salt, mineral oil, potpourri oil and food coloring. Stir until mixed well. The mixture will be damp but grainy. Put in cellophane bag, tie with raffia and add a gift tag that says, "Add 3 heaping spoonfuls to a warm bath."

Place bag in clay pot, invert saucer to become a lid and tie with a raffia bow.

Things You'll Need:

1 cup Epsom salts
2 Tablespoons Mineral oil
3 drops food coloring
4" Terra Cotta clay pot and saucer
Acrylic paints
1" foam brush
Kitchen sponge cut into shape of a heart
Cellophane bag
Clear spray varnish
Wax paper
Raffia
Gift tag
Scissors

Notes

Summer

Blue skies. . . Bright days. . . Warm walks in the early evening. . . Twilight. . . Kids yawning at noontime. . . Breakfast for lunch. . . Beach balls and seahorses. . . We've cruised through the seasons to summer! Oh, but there's nothing quite like it: "Let's play. . . it's the good ole summertime!"

Things You'll Need:

15-20 photographs of
    you and your dad
Wooden serving tray
Scissors
Glue
Decoupage Medium
Two sponge brushes
    (one for paint and
    one for glue)
Acrylic paints of your
    choice
Stencils (optional)

I owe almost
everything to
my father.

Margaret Thatcher

Dad's Day Tray

Pick out 15-20 of your favorite photos of you, your dad and your family. If possible, they should be pictures that bring back the best memories. Take the photos to a copy center and have them make color copies of each picture. Try to get as many pictures on one 8½ by 11 sheet as possible to cut down on costs.

Paint the inside of the tray with the acrylic paints you've selected and let dry. Paint the outside of the tray another color and let dry. You will want to be especially careful at the edges where the two colors meet.

While you are waiting for the tray to dry, cut out your pictures. You may want to cut them in a variety of shapes using a stencil or just freehand them. You can also add words or phrases that you have cut out of magazines that remind you of your dad.

Practice laying the photos and words out in the dry tray to get an idea of what you want. Carefully glue the backs of the photos to the tray. If you are using a white glue (like Elmer's), water it down a bit before starting. Make sure the edges have glue around them. If any of the photos overlap, be sure to glue the bottom photos down first.

When the glue has dried, paint a coat of decoupage medium over the entire surface of the tray to seal it. Repeat with the decoupage when the first coat is dry, but this time cover the entire tray. Allow to dry.

Fix your dad's favorite snack, take him to his favorite chair and share some fun memories together.

Sunflower Fort

Summer memories are made up of barefoot walks, swimming, lazy days outside, quiet nights catching fireflies, and secret hideaways where we can store up our dreams.

With a bit of preplanning and care, you can have a special place that can be a secret hideaway or the neighborhood clubhouse. Ask your parents if there is a small flat piece of land for you to use for your special getaway. The land should be in an open spot so the sunflowers can grow without interference from taller trees.

Things You'll Need:

Sunflower seeds in
two heights
Gardening tools
Measuring tape
Watering can

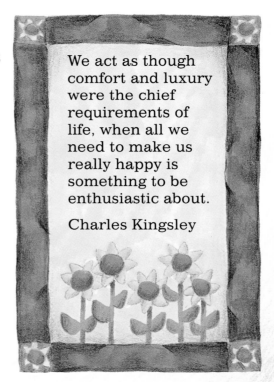

We act as though comfort and luxury were the chief requirements of life, when all we need to make us really happy is something to be enthusiastic about.

Charles Kingsley

Purchase different varieties of sunflower seed packets where the mature flowers are two different heights. One height should be approximately 6-8 feet tall. Using a stick, draw out a horseshoe design on the ground in the size you have planned for your getaway. Be sure to allow space for a three foot opening (this is the "doorway" into your fort). Plant the seeds according to the package directions on spacing and watering, alternating the two sizes of flowers.

With plenty of care and patience (lots of that), your secret place will be ready for you to disappear to just when you really need it.

FAR FROM THE CROWD

Far from the crowd I will pick my way,
    Apart from society,
For I must pause and rest awhile
    And find a trail for me.

So push and climb on your noisy way;
    I choose a different goal,
To nestle in my quiet place
    And grow within my soul.

          Viola Berg

As a child I loved to hear the distant sound of the bell ringing out from the ice cream truck.

My brother, sister and I would rush through the house collecting change and the occasional dollar bill as if our entire future depended on our greeting the ice cream truck as it beckoned us to come out before it passed by.

It was an annual summertime tradition. We would hurry to swallow each bite in the summer heat. Then we would play the evening away until our parents would call us home for baths and bed.

The ice cream truck may be but a fond memory for most of us, but ice cream still calls out to me. If I am still enough, I can hear the bell of the ice cream truck in the distance.

"Shake, Rattle and Roll" Ice Cream

In the smaller coffee can, combine half-and-half, sugar, and vanilla; stir well. Put the lid on tightly and secure it with duck tape. Place a thin layer of crushed ice on the bottom of the larger coffee can; sprinkle with 1 tablespoon rock salt. Place the small can inside the large can. Pack the area between the cans with crushed ice and rock salt using about 2 tablespoons rock salt for every cup of ice. Put lid tightly on the large can and secure it with duck tape.

Roll the can back and forth for about 10 to 15 minutes on the sidewalk or porch. If it's too hot outside you can do this on a countertop inside but be sure to put a towel down to protect the surface.

Lift out smaller can and carefully remove lid. Scrape down sides and stir all the ice cream together. (If the ice cream is too soft, repack large can with fresh rock salt and ice; replace lid. Roll back and forth a few minutes more until firm).

You will have about five ½ cup servings to share with your friends.

Things You'll Need:

One large (2 lb., 7 oz.) coffee can with lid
One 1 lb. coffee can with lid
1 pint half-and-half
½ cup sugar
1 teaspoon vanilla
Crushed ice (6 to 7 cups)
Rock salt (about ¾ cup)
Duck tape

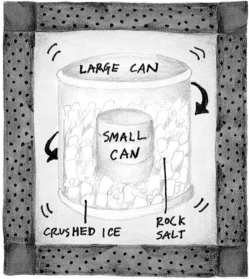

LARGE CAN

SMALL CAN

CRUSHED ICE   ROCK SALT

Things You'll Need:
Round oatmeal
  container
Window screen or
  mesh
Ruler
Acrylic Paint
Paintbrush
Stickers
Scissors
Clear Tape
Small branches,
  wood chips, grass
  or other natural
  habitat

A Bug's World

Cut out the middle of an oatmeal container, leaving about 2" at the top and bottom. Keep the lid on the box.

Cut a piece of window screen or mesh the same size as the section of the box that was cut out.

Paint the bottom, top, and back with acrylic paint and allow to dry. Decorate with stickers if you like.

Attach the screen to the outside edges of "window" with tape. Be careful not to cut yourself with the rough edges of the screen. Place small branches, wood chips, grass and other habitat material inside.

Remove the lid to put insects inside so that you can observe their world.

Dream your dreams, then blueprint your dreams and finally contract with yourself to construct them, stone by stone, but while you are dreaming, dream big!

Guilford Dudley, Jr.

© Debi Hron

You meet a new friend and you want to jot her a note. With a little creativity you can personalize your own note cards (that will get a "thumbs up")!

Plan what design you want to make out of your thumbprint. You may want to start with something simple at first, like a ladybug. Then advance to more difficult things as you gain more experience.

Thumbs Up! Stationery

Pour a small amount of red paint on a plastic plate. Gently put your thumb in the paint so that it is wet but not too thick. Lightly place your thumb on the paper, going around the edges, making sure to space "bugs" evenly. When the paint begins to get light on the paper, dip your thumb in the paint again. Do the same thing along the bottom edge of the envelope, front and back. Allow to dry.

With a black pen, draw a line down the center of the ladybug's back. Give her a black face and polka dots. Once you've mastered your ladybug note cards, try making other animals or flowers or (whatever you can think of)!

Think of seven people who have encouraged you in some way or another. Write a note to each one on your new stationery, thanking them for their words or deeds. Send a note every day this week. Next week, think of seven people you can encourage, and send a note to each of them.

Things You'll Need:

White note cards and envelopes (card stock weight paper available at office supply stores)
Red acrylic paint
Black permanent marker
Plastic plate

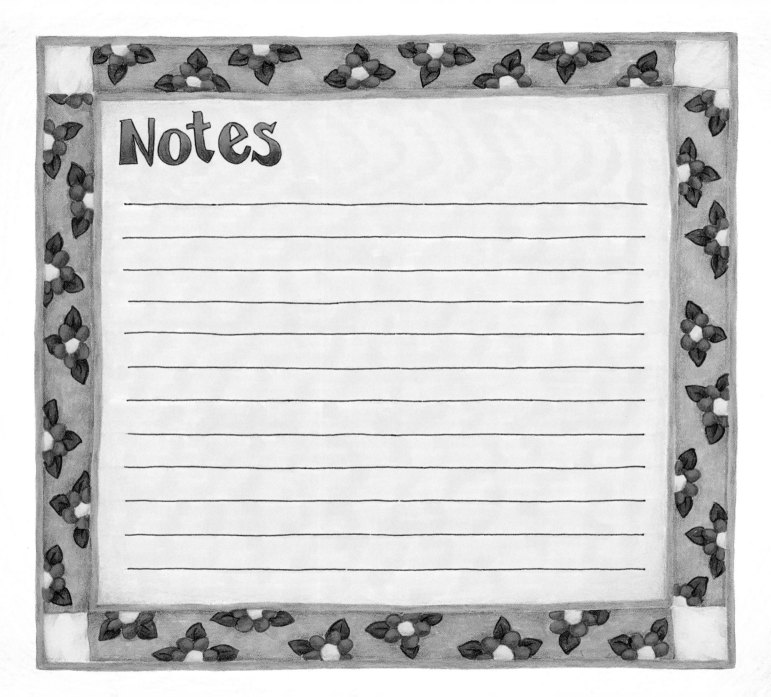

Notes

_____

_____

_____

_____

_____

_____

_____

_____

_____

Autumn

We continue our journey with a crisp morning walk and take in the smell of a warm fireplace. We enjoy the newly painted landscapes. We cannot pass too quickly through Autumn, for we may be in danger of missing the tiniest delight to our senses. Pause and rest awhile with us. Life is good!

Painted skies
Lofty dreams,
Dare to reach
On
Golden wings.

A Pocket Full of Purses

Cut out the back pocket and the jean material behind the pocket from an old pair of jeans. The pocket and pants should be free of all holes. Cut carefully outside the seams so the pocket stays in one piece.

With a needle and thread, sew the ribbon, braid or belt onto the sides of the pocket to make a shoulder strap. Adjust the shoulder strap to your height (a yard is a good approximate length).

Things You'll Need:

An old pair of blue jeans
One yard of ribbon
Needle and thread
Scissors
Iron-on transfers, fabric paint,
   beads, buttons, etc.
Velcro strips

Let your creative energy go wild on the outside of the pocket. You can make a retro purse by adding smiley-face iron-on transfers or any other 70's applique look. Fabric paints, beads, or buttons are just a few of the items you could use to decorate the pocket.

Sew strips of Velcro to the inside of the pocket to hold the purse shut. You will be looking for an excuse to "wear" your old jeans again!

Candy Corn Pots

Things You'll Need:

3" clay pot
White acrylic paint
Yellow acrylic paint
Orange acrylic paint
Black acrylic paint
Thin line paint brush
1" sponge brush
⅜" unfinished
   wooden button
   (found in craft
   stores)
Clear acrylic sealer
Glue

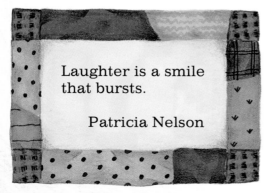

Laughter is a smile
that bursts.

Patricia Nelson

Nothing reminds me of the coming autumn season quite like the sight of the familiar bags of candy corn at my local market. Just as mysteriously as they appear, they disappear again, the day after Halloween (where do those imps hide!)

Enjoy them while you can and make a festive container to hold them.

Paint the clay pot white, inside and out, and set aside to dry. Repeat. Paint the top rim of the pot yellow and the middle, orange. Leave the bottom 1" white. Give the orange and yellow a second coat. Let dry completely. Paint the wooden button yellow.

Paint eyes and a mouth on the pot following the example. Add a white accent mark on the "button nose". Glue the nose on and allow to dry. Spray two coats of the sealer on, allowing to dry between coats.

Fill with candy!

Ways to jazz up your room:

❀ Paint 3" clay pots to put your pens, pencils, and markers in.

❀ Add colorful trim to your lampshade.

❀ Keep lots of picture frames and update the photos often.

❀ Make some throw pillows for your bed.

❀ Store your odds and ends in decorative boxes.

Noteworthy Art

Things You'll Need:

Two same-size cardboard frames from center of fabric bolts (found in fabric stores)
Batting
1 yard fabric
Ribbon
½" Decorative upholstery tacks
Scissors
Duct tape
Glue gun and glue sticks

A real friend is one who walks in when the rest of the world walks out.

Walter Winchell

Tape the two cardboard bolts together, like the picture below. Be sure to tape them together securely. Lay the bolts on top of the batting. Cut the batting 2" larger than the cardboard. Carefully glue the batting to the back of the cardboard.

Lay the fabric down on the cutting surface, wrong side up. Center the cardboard on the fabric. Cut the fabric 2½" larger than the cardboard. Begin on the short side and glue the fabric to the back of the cardboard. As you glue each side, pull the fabric tightly, but evenly, so it is taut in the front.

Cut another piece of fabric the size of the cardboard plus 1½". Fold the extra 1½" in and glue to keep it in place. Set aside.

Measure the ribbon diagonally on the fabric-covered board like the picture. Add 4" and place on front of the board. Glue on back of the board, making sure the ribbon is tight across the front. Wherever the ribbons cross, place an upholstery tack. You might want to add a dot of hot glue under each tack before sticking it to the fabric and cardboard.

Cut two 2" pieces of ribbon and make loops. Glue each loop on the top back corners. Cover the back with the other piece of fabric, taking care with the glue gun.

Now you're ready to hang your noteworthy art in your room to show off some of your prized papers!

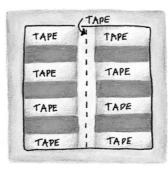

© Debi Hron

Autumn - the Work of the Imps?
Donna L. Valverde

In the blink of an eye
all the green leaves turn
yellow, and orange, and red.
(And where do those imps find
paint brushes?)
Then swift as lightning
The leaves color brown,
and are plucked off each branch,
one-by-one,
If an ear is tuned-
giggles pass in the breeze, and
crisp leaves somehow(?)
stack into piles.

And the moon swells round
and the air is brisk,
and the nights-
Nights abound with
their play.
And the children are pulled
from the bright warmth of home
to frolic in costume and dress.
Cats land on fences,
silhouetting the moon
As jack-o-lanterns
Grin ear-to-ear.
Trick, or Treat??

Tricks with Treats

Pumpkins are everywhere during the autumn months. You can create your own style of pumpkin, using a one gallon can.

If there is a label on the can, peel it off. Have an adult help you sand down any rough edges. Wash and dry the can.

Spray paint the can, inside and outside, with yellow spray paint and allow to dry. Apply another coat of spray paint and allow to dry.

Wet your sponge in the water. Squeeze out water so the sponge is damp, not wet. Dip the sponge in the orange acrylic paint, covering the outside of the can. Allow to dry.

Draw a jack-o-lantern face on the can with a pencil, following the sample. Paint the face on the can, using black for the eyes and mouth. Paint the nose red. Paint two small white dots in the eyes, using the tip of the paintbrush handle, dipped in white paint. With a permanent black marker, draw corners of the mouth, outline the nose and draw eyebrows. For the cheeks, thin the red paint with water and sponge lightly around the corners of the mouth.

For the handle, have an adult make a hole on each side of the can near the top, using a hammer, nail and a block of wood to reinforce the can while hammering. Thread the wire through the holes. Leave about 2 inches outside of each hole. Curl the wire ends by wrapping around a pencil.

If you like, add a raffia bow and cut out a large square of orange cellophane. Place the cellophane inside the can, fill the can with your favorite fall treats and share your gift of friendship with someone else.

Things You'll Need:

One gallon can (a large coffee can from the school cafeteria would work great)
Yellow spray paint
Acrylic paints (orange, black, red, white)
One 30" length 18 gauge wire
Wire cutters
Black permanent marker for outlining
Small paintbrush
Sponge
Hammer and nail
Block of wood
Pencil
Raffia (optional)
Orange cellophane (optional)

Things You'll Need:

One 5" x 7" unfinished
  wooden craft frame
  (available at craft
  stores)
Paint markers -
  medium and fine
  point
Clear acrylic sealant
Metal screening
  (available by the
  foot at hardware
  stores)
Wire cutters
Ribbon
Two upholstery tacks
Four teacup hooks
  (that screw in)
Scissors
Glue gun and glue
  sticks

The first duty of
love is to listen.

Paul Tillech

Picture This

Dress up your room with a decorative frame that doubles as a handy spot for your earrings and necklaces.

Jazz up your unfinished frame with the paint markers. You can write your name, paint stripes or be as creative as you want to be. Coordinate colors with your room. Put two coats of clear sealant over the front and let dry.

Cut the metal screening with the wire cutters to fit in the center of the frame. It would be better for the screening to be a bit too big rather than risk it being too small. It should fit securely on the lip of the frame opening. Use the glue gun and glue the screen onto the lip, one side at a time.

Measure the top side of the frame plus 3" for the ribbon hanger. Fasten the ribbon using the upholstery tacks. Screw the teacup hooks on the top front, two on each side.

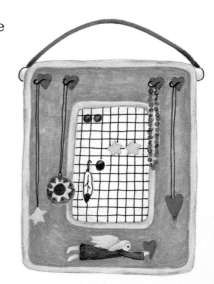

You are now ready to decorate your frame with all of your favorite earrings and necklaces!

When there is room
in the heart, there is
room in the house.

Danish Proverb

©Debi Hron

Hand Dipped Candle

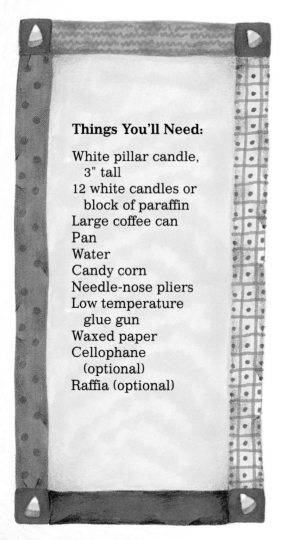

Things You'll Need:

White pillar candle,
   3" tall
12 white candles or
   block of paraffin
Large coffee can
Pan
Water
Candy corn
Needle-nose pliers
Low temperature
   glue gun
Waxed paper
Cellophane
   (optional)
Raffia (optional)

Ask an adult to help you with this craft.

Fill a pan ⅓ full of water. Place the pan on the stove burner over low heat. Put the candles or paraffin in the coffee can and place in the pan on the stove. Be sure and stay in the kitchen while the candles are melting to make sure the wax doesn't get too hot!

While the wax is melting, carefully glue the candy corn to the bottom ⅓ of the pillar candle. Always use caution when using a glue gun.

Remove the candle wicks from the coffee can with a fork when the wax has melted. Grab the pillar candle by its wick using needle nose pliers and slowly dip into the melted wax, covering all the candies and up to the top of the pillar. Bring out of the wax and let dry on waxed paper. Repeat the dipping process three or four times until the candle is coated, as you like.

Be sure to remove the coffee can from the stove as soon as you are done and turn the burner off.

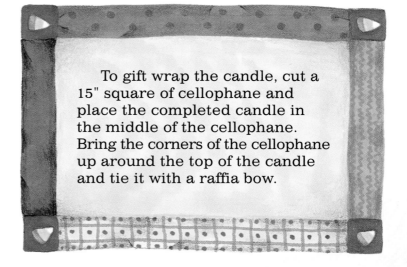

To gift wrap the candle, cut a 15" square of cellophane and place the completed candle in the middle of the cellophane. Bring the corners of the cellophane up around the top of the candle and tie it with a raffia bow.

Notes

_____

_____

_____

_____

_____

_____

_____

_____

_____

_____

Winter

My favorite part of winter is the stillness. After the busy holidays, I welcome a rest. Bears take long winter naps. . . Maybe we should, too. Enjoy the stillness of winter before journeying on.

Winter Warmer Mug

As a child, on cold winter mornings, my mom would wake me up by saying, "The cold north wind's gonna be nippin' at your toes." Now, as I wake my children up with that same saying on blustery days, we often have hot chocolate before they head off to school, just as I did. This makes a great Christmas gift for a teacher or your favorite sledding buddy. Hot chocolate is a must after a day of sledding!

To make the mug, design your picture on paper before you begin. You can use a Christmas design or a winter scene such as a snowman. Paint that design on your mug. Paint the handle to look like a candy cane, if desired. Follow manufacturer's instructions to cure the paint. The mugs are dishwasher safe, according to the paint manufacturer, but I would hand wash.

Recipe for hot cocoa mix
(print this neatly on a small card and include with the mix)
Measure 3 tablespoons of mix into mug. Add 6-8 ozs. of hot water, stirring until smooth.

To make the spoons, microwave the chocolate almond bark following package directions. Dip the spoon into the melted chocolate so that the spoon is covered up to about ¼ of the handle. Carefully place the dipped spoon on the baking sheet covered with waxed paper. When the chocolate has hardened, place spoon inside plastic bag and tie with the ribbon.

To make the Cocoa mix, combine all of the ingredients in a large bowl. Pour into the plastic storage bag and tie with ribbon. Store any remaining mix in an airtight container.

If you are giving all three items as a gift, place the cocoa mix and two spoons inside the mug. Be sure and include the recipe for hot cocoa.

Things You'll Need:

Mugs:
Plain ceramic mug
DecoArt ULTRA GLOSS acrylic enamel paint

Cocoa Mix:
8½ cups nonfat dry milk
1½ cups (6 oz. jar) nondairy creamer
3 cups instant chocolate drink mix for milk
1½ cups confectioner's sugar
1½ cups miniature marshmallows
Clear plastic storage bag
Curling ribbon

Spoons:
Chocolate flavored almond bark
Heavy-duty plastic spoons (red or green)
Curling ribbon
Scissors
Plastic lollipop bags
Waxed paper
Baking sheet

We are all travelers in
the wilderness of this
world, and the best that
we find in our travels is
an honest friend.

Robert Louis Stevenson

This Little Piggy Went to Market

Trace your feet on the cardboard and cut out. Place the cardboard feet into the socks so they are flat against the soles of the socks. Paint a design of your choice on the sock bottoms. Squeeze the paint straight from the bottle if it has a small tip. Be sure and shake the covered bottle often so that there are no air bubbles trapped inside.

Let the paint dry overnite before removing the cardboard or wearing the socks. If you want to add designs on the other parts of the socks, go ahead. Be sure to put cardboard inside the socks so the paint doesn't bleed onto other areas. Wait about three days to machine-wash and dry your socks.

Things You'll Need:

Cotton socks
   (prewashed)
Cardboard
Pencil
Scissors
3-dimensional paint
   (found in craft
   stores)

For the Birds

The generosity of the Christmas season can extend past people and out into nature. . . Help your parents haul your very dry (and now lonely looking) Christmas tree outside and stand it upright. Be sure to help clean up the mess the dry needles may have made inside. Begin decorating your tree, only this time decorate it for the birds.

Thread cereal, popcorn or cranberries on string and drape around the tree for garland. Dip pretzels in peanut butter and then roll them in birdseed for easy edible ornaments. With cookie cutters, cut out shapes from bread. Spread peanut butter on one side and cover with sunflower seeds. Poke a hole in the top and hang with a string.

Things You'll Need:

Bread
Cookie cutters
Peanut butter
Butter knife
String
Scissors
Oranges
Cutting knife
Spoon
Cereal
Pretzels
Popcorn
Cranberries
Birdseed

Recycling your tree can serve two purposes: to feed the birds over the cold winter, and to give them shelter.

Oranges make good ornaments also. Carefully cut an orange in half. Scoop out the fruit to the rind. Put two holes at the top, equally spaced and tie a 9" piece of string through the holes, knotting at each end. Fill with birdseed and hang on the tree.

In no time, your old tree will look lovely again and the birds will be enjoying your gift.

The inhabitants of cities suppose that the country landscape is pleasant only half the year. I please myself with the graces of the winter scenery, and believe that we are as much touched by it as by the genial influences of summer. To the attentive eye, each moment of the year has its own beauty, and in the same field, it beholds, every hour, a picture which was never seen before and which will never be seen again.

Ralph Waldo Emerson

Snowman's Closet

I always love the first snowfall. Large flakes quietly floating down. . . The best snow for building the perfect snowman is not too wet, not to dry.

Your snowman deserves a special place for his clothes. Why not make him a "closet" to store his clothes and accessories in?

Paint your box white and let it dry. Paint the sides of the bottom and the sides of the lid blue. Paint a snowman's face, including a hat on the top of the lid. Set it aside to dry. Paint snowflakes around the side of the bottom and write "Snowman's Closet" with your white paint marker.

Look around the house for all the "makings" of a snowman. All you will need to complete his outfit is a carrot, twigs for arms and snow!

Things You'll Need:

10" round paper
   maché box or any
   box with lid
Acrylic paints
Paint brushes
   (1" foam brush and
   smaller brushes)
Bowl of water
Paper towels
Old scarf
Old hat
Gloves or mittens
Several pieces of
   charcoal (store in a
   plastic bag)
Large buttons or
   rocks
White medium point
   paint marker

The family
is
one of nature's
masterpieces.

~George Santayana

Snap, Crackle and Pop!

There is nothing like ringing in the New Year with a little fun. Whether you get together with friends or play games at home with your family, "crackers" will be a hit. "Crackers" are English party favors, most often used during the holiday season. But they can be adapted for any time of the year.

Cut cardboard paper towel tubes 5" long. Place the small gifts, candies, confetti, etc. inside the tube. Leave enough room inside so the contents can move around.

Cover the tube in tissue paper and tie the ends with ribbon. You can add a contrasting square of tissue if you would like to add more color. Add stickers, rickrack, or fancy edged paper to add pizzazz to your cracker. Shred the ends to give it a more festive feel.

If you are giving these as gifts, use a gold marker and add the names of your guests. Now you are ready to celebrate any occasion in style!

Things You'll Need:

Paper towel tubes
Tissue paper
  (or wrapping
  paper)
Ribbon
Scissors
Glue
Stickers
Rickrack
Small goodies or
  treats

Make new friends, but keep the old. One is silver, the other is gold.

Babysitter's Treasure Box

Place the contact paper, front side down, on the surface you will be cutting on. Place the box bottom on top of it. Measure all 4 sides plus an additional 3". Cut out the contact paper to your measurements and make cuts where the side "seams" should be. Carefully peel away the paper to reveal the sticky side of the contact paper. Start from the bottom and smooth out the air bubbles with your hand as you go up. Turn the excess contact paper inside the box and secure it with your hand. Do the same on the other side. On the long sides, after you bring each side up, wrap the excess contact paper around the two sides. Repeat the same process with the top.

Paint or write "Babysitter's Treasure Box" along the top of your box. Decorate the box with stickers, pictures, or whatever you like.

Some suggestions for treasures to store inside the box are: old adult clothes, hats and shoes for dress up, discarded jewelry, coloring books and crayons, children's scissors, construction paper, glue sticks, Old Maid or Go Fish cards, and whatever you can think of that the children you are babysitting would consider a special treat for you to bring along.

Things You'll Need:

Storage box
 (available at office
 supply stores) with
 lid and at least 24"
 by 15"
Contact paper
Stickers
Pictures from
 magazines
Glue Scissors
Tulip paints
Your treasures for
 inside the box

Adventure is
where you find it,
and you can find
it anywhere.

Notes